CW00665541

ALEX BOYD FRSA is a photographer, curator and writer based in the west of Scotland. Until recently he lived in the Outer Hebrides. His work has been widely exhibited internationally with solo exhibitions at the Scottish Parliament, as well as group exhibitions at the Royal Academy, the Royal Ulster Academy and the Royal Scottish Academy. His work is held in the collections of the National Galleries of Scotland, the Royal Photographic Society, the Royal Scottish Academy, the V&A and the Yale Centre for British Art in the US. His first book, *St Kilda: The Silent Islands,* was shortlisted for the Saltire Society First Book Award in 2018. He is a contributing arts editor for the *Island Review* and *Art North.* He is currently undertaking a PhD on Scottish photography.

JONATHAN MEADES is a writer, journalist, essayist and filmmaker. His books include three works of fiction and several anthologies, including *Museum Without Walls*, which received 13 nominations as a book of the year in 2012. *An Encyclopaedia of Myself* won Best Memoir in the Spear's Book Awards 2014 and was shortlisted for the 2015 Pen Ackerley Prize. Meades has written and performed in more than 50 television shows on predominantly topographical subjects such as shacks, garden cities and megastructures. He is currently working on a film about Franco. His most recently broadcast film was *Jonathan Meades on Jargon* (BBC Four), described in *The Guardian* as 'blisteringly brutal, clever and hilarious'.

DAN HICKS FSA, MCIfA is Professor of Contemporary Archaeology at the University of Oxford, Curator at the Pitt Rivers Museum, and a Fellow of St Cross College, Oxford. Dan teaches Archaeology, Anthropology and History of Art at Oxford, and he has written widely about the intersections between these three fields. Dan has published seven books to date, most recently *Lande: The Calais 'Jungle' and Beyond* (Bristol University Press 2019, with Sarah Mallet) and *Archaeology and Photography: Time, Objectivity and Archive* (Bloomsbury 2019, edited with Lesley McFadyen). In 2019 he did his first ever comedy gig in London, with comedian Mark Thomas.

By the same author:

St Kilda: The Silent Islands, Luath, 2018
Hirta: A Portrait of St Kilda, Luath, 2019

Isle of Rust

A Portrait of Lewis and Harris

ALEX BOYD

with

Jonathan Meades and Dan Hicks

Luath Press Limited

EDINBURGH

www.luath.co.uk

First published 2019
Reprinted 2020

ISBN: 978-1-913025-00-7

The authors' right to be identified as author of this book
under the Copyright, Designs and Patents Act 1988 has been asserted.

The paper used in this book is recyclable. It is made
from low chlorine pulps produced in a low energy,
low emission manner from renewable forests.

Printed and bound by
iPrint Global Ltd., Ely.

Typeset in 10.5 point Sabon by Main Point Books, Edinburgh

Contents

Acknowledgements

ALEX BOYD would like to thank the following people for their help in the creation of this book. Firstly Jonathan Meades for his fine essay; his writings and contributions are a constant source of inspiration. Thank you also to Professor Dan Hicks for his wonderful Afterword. Thanks also to the many people who helped to make Lewis our home for several years, from Anne Campbell and Jon MacLeod who first guided me across the landscape, to the team at An Lanntair, who made it a home. Special mention to Elly Fletcher, Roddy Murray, Paula Brown and Joe Mahony who make the island a better place through their tireless work. Thank you to all those who allowed me to photograph them, I wish I could have included you all here. Thank you to Barbara Ziehm, Sam and Caroline, and Eve and Andrea, the kindest people I know – your friendship and enthusiasm during those long winter months kept us going, and this book is dedicated to you. Thank you to Pearse O'Halloran, and the team at Luath, especially Maia Gentle, Lauren Grieve and Gavin MacDougall. Heartfelt thanks to Jennie Renton and Coreen Grant at Main Point Books, who worked tirelessly to make the book happen. Finally thank you to my wife, Jessica. Der Liebe ist kein Wind zu kalt.

JONATHAN MEADES would like to thank the following people who worked on *The Isle of Rust*, the BBC film from whose script the essay has been adapted: Colin Murray, director; Alastair McCormick, director of photography; Allan Campbell, series producer.

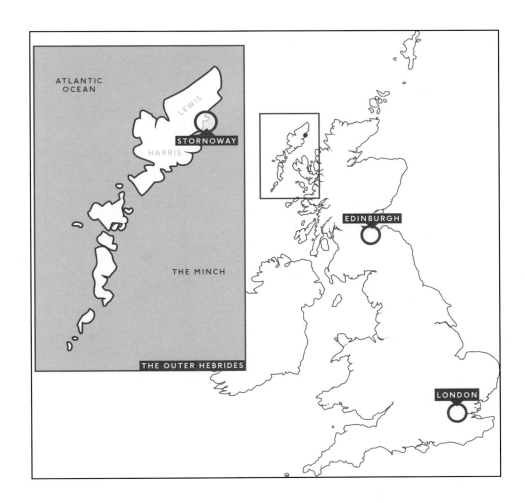

ATLANTIC
OCEAN

LEWIS

STORNOWAY

HARRIS

THE MINCH

THE OUTER HEBRIDES

EDINBURGH

LONDON

Harris landscape, Kendebig, Harris

Two Winters and Three Summers on Lewis

Alex Boyd

THERE ARE MANY names for the island known as Lewis and Harris (Leòdhas agus na Hearadh), from the poetic the Heather Isle (Eilean an Fhraoich) to the more prosaic the Long Island (an t-Eilean Fada). A few islanders – no doubt affectionately – refer to the third largest island in the British Isles as The Rock. It is a name that does this most diverse of landscapes and habitats something of a disservice, as it so much more than just an outcrop of metamorphic gneiss, granite, basalt and sandstone on the Atlantic edge of Europe.

To my mind, no sobriquet is more apt than that given over a decade ago by Jonathan Meades, who provided us with the title *Isle of Rust* in his landmark BBC film of the same name. This name, of course, not only refers to the countless corroding tractors, weaving sheds and other visible signs of human settlement but also to the colours of the land: the reds of deergrass and the purple moor grass which make up so much of the moorland. It is a place of great contrast in both light and land, from the largely flat peatlands of Lewis, where the majority of islanders make their home, to the mountains of Harris that rise abruptly in the south, marking out the rocky landscapes so different to the north of the island.

It is in settlements nestled in bays and natural harbours or stretched out along seemingly endless coastal roads that Scotland's largest concentration of Gaelic speakers can be found. It is a place where old traditions such as peat cutting, weaving and crofting sit alongside the modern demands of island life.

I grew up in the Lowlands of Scotland and until I went there, I thought of the Outer Hebrides as being on the edge of the periphery, a place of barren windswept landscapes, of fishing fleets riding high seas, of croft houses and pristine white beaches – a place which had very little in common with the ordered and picturesque farmlands of my native Ayrshire and the once thriving but now rapidly declining coastal towns of the west of Scotland.

The opportunity to visit the islands of the northwest would largely elude me until 2013, when I was offered the role of Artist-in-Residence with the Royal Scottish Academy on the Isle of Skye. Based in a studio at the University of the Highlands and Islands at Sabhal Mór Ostaig, I got my first glimpses of the Outer Hebrides while climbing along the Trotternish Ridge in the north of the island, looking west and observing a long archipelago skirting the horizon.

It was a commission to make artwork about the peatlands of Lewis that summer which finally provided me with the chance to experience first-hand the islands I had come to know largely through the eyes of photographers such as Werner Kissling, Margaret Fay Shaw, Gus Wylie and Paul Strand. I had also recently seen Jonathan Meades' beautiful and bleak *Isle of Rust*. His vision of Lewis and Harris provided the inspiration for a new series of work which would combine an antique camera, chemicals and rust collected from the land.

Leaving Skye to cross the calm waters of the Minch, that great sense of the unknown was further enhanced by Leaving Skye to cross the calm waters of the Minch, that great sense of the unknown was further enhanced by the play of the light – crepuscular rays of light breaking through black clouds and illuminating the Shiant islands to the north. Home to dramatic volcanic columns which bring to mind Staffa or the Giant's Causeway, they rose from the depths like broken teeth.

Arriving in the harbour at Tarbert on Harris, I drove south, gaining my first impressions of the island as I climbed high over the pass dominated by the Clisham, the highest mountain in the archipelago and part of the range which separates Harris from Lewis. Before the introduction of the road which winds its way over hills and around boulders and lochs, this was once a journey made by sea, explaining why this single landmass has two separate and distinct communities.

As I passed Loch Seaforth and the communities of South Lochs, and onward through the village of Ballalan, the rocky terrain gradually gave way to the wider moorland expanses of Lewis and it wasn't long before I arrived in the harbour town of Stornoway where I would stay for the night.

The next morning began with an early start. I made my way across the winding moorland road to the village of Bragar, where I met local artist and archeologist Anne Campbell. We drove on together to Ness and my first introduction to the Lewis peatlands. We were joined by Anne's enthusiastic border collie, Bran, who ran ahead of us, stopping only to dig in the mud and occasionally bark at his own reflection in the many pools of water which made up this unfamiliar landscape. In the distance, we observed only a few lonely figures out gathering peat.

As we made our way deeper into the moor,

with the clouds low and dark above and a feature-less horizon beyond, I started to feel a slight sense of oppression, peculiar in such an open landscape. Perhaps it was partly to do with being disorientated, the damp and humid conditions or my first encounter with Lewis's many insects that flew curiously around us, occasionally biting.

Lining the sides of the road I noticed the many peat banks stretching out towards the water's edge, the marks of the shovels still apparent. Above them, small stacks of peat awaited collection, laid out in herringbone patterns or scattered around the landscape in rows. Further up the track, we examined peat cut by machine, which, instead of having a pleasing briquette form, was heaped up in piles of cracked and broken cylinders due to being bored from the land. Having seen the industrial-scale destruction that such machines have wrought on the moors of Ireland, Anne and I remarked that they should be banned entirely from the moor.

As we began to gain height, we could see the peat road dropping below to reveal a small valley dotted with an eclectic range of buildings: the shieling village of Cuidhsiadar, our destination.

Cuidhsiadar is the site of a practice once integral to island life: transhumance. Islanders would take animals out to graze on the moorland in summer, living there and collecting produce such as milk and butter, which would then help sustain them through the harsh winter months. Structures used to house people here over hundreds of years are now reduced to piles of stones. Around them are scattered a selection of much more contemporary huts, several constructed from tin and some simple wooden dwellings in various states of disrepair.

In the far distance, we could see a much older turf-covered structure on the moor, but it was a modern shieling in front of us which drew the most attention. From beneath wooden panels, the vague form of one of the tour buses which used to cross the island could be discerned, gutted and then converted into a makeshift home on the moor. Open to the elements, we headed inside it for shelter and between the upholstery we noticed beds, as well as bags of peat still to be processed. The ingenuity of islanders to re-use and re-purpose items which would long since have been consigned to the scrapheap elsewhere is something I would see again and again.

Following a few days of exploring the island, visiting familiar tourist landmarks such as the standing stones of Callanish, the Broch at Dun Carloway and many journeys back and forward over the Pentland moor road, I started to get a better idea of the landscape that I was working within.

Staying in a small post-war croft house in Anne's home village of Bragar, I began to appreciate the vastness of the moor, the complete absence of trees. Visible from my kitchen window, the North Atlantic stretching uninterrupted to the west. It is an environment where individuals are quietly reminded of their place; of their own smallness in comparison to the sheer vastness of the natural world around them. It is a feeling often lost in towns and cities.

My own experience of moorland had previously been limited to my own wanderings around the south-west of Scotland and my work as a photographer on the vastness of Rannoch Moor, an area claimed to be one of the last true wild places by writers such as Robert Macfarlane, who Anne had guided across the moors of Lewis. Anne had recently published a beautiful collection called *Rathad an Isein* (*The Bird's Road*), a moorland glossary which she had collected along with her sister Catriona, Finlay Macleod and Donald Morrisson. It gives a unique insight into how the moorland is viewed in the Gaelic imagination and experience and includes terms used by those who have worked and cut peat on the moors for many generations. Her offer to accompany me on a walk across the Lewis peatland and to spend a night in her family shieling at the heart of the island was one I immediately agreed to.

In the days leading up to the walk, the weather shifted from sunny and pleasant to increasingly cloudy conditions. A change was in the air. As is not unusual on these islands, weather and storm warnings became the main topic of conversation but we decided that we would make the trip out onto the moor regardless. We could only hope that the wind and rain would stay away long enough for us to reach the shieling on the slopes of Beinn a' Chanaich Mhoir, by the waters of Loch nan Leac.

Looking at an OS map our destination seemed remarkably close – only five or six miles away – but with the ground waterlogged and marshy, every step promised to be a torturous effort. The next morning, with a heavy rucksack laden with a camera, food and camping equipment and the prospect of terrible weather and harsh terrain, I still felt energised and enthusiastic about the challenge to come.

Leaving the car at the end of the track, I joined Anne and Bran, and we began to make our way along the drowned peat road towards the moor. Our path would follow along the course of the Abhainn Arnol, a shallow river which runs the length of Glen Bragar. To our right loomed Beinn Choinnich (the Hill of Kenneth) while in the distance, the distinctive pyramid form of Stacashal kept my eyes fixed on the horizon.

Passing men loading dry peat into the back of tractors, my eye was caught by something small, box-like and metallic at the edge of the riverbank. On closer inspection, Anne informed me that it was

Summer shielings, Cuishader, Ness, Lewis

The open moorlands of Lewis from Achmore.

Solar powered shieling, Ness, Lewis

Shieling village, Cuishader, Ness, Lewis

a trap for mink, which, along with hedgehogs, were introduced to the island in the 1950s and '60s. The mink caused widespread damage to the birds of the moorland and it is only now that many of them are beginning to return in number to the moor. The story emphasises the fragile balance which often exists in such places.

Our next pause on the moor was signalled by an excited bark from Bran, who started digging furiously into the peat. Anne explained that we had arrived at her own peat field and that Bran was simply imitating the actions of Anne and her sister, who still dig peat to warm their homes. It was on this site that Anne, whilst digging into a peat bank, found a wooden bowl, the earth giving it up after holding on to it for over a millennium. It was one of undoubtedly many thousands of objects that the moor has held onto, waiting for an archaeologist such as Anne to uncover it and learn something of the people who once made their home there.

It is unfortunate that, unlike the well-excavated and fascinating Céide Fields in the north-west of the Republic of Ireland, little archaeological research has gone into the north of Lewis, an area obviously rich in potential finds. It was this frustration which led Anne to return to university to study archaeology. As part of her Masters dissertation, she walked the land and recorded finds. What she uncovered added hugely to existing knowledge, yet there is still more work to be done. Whatever lies beneath the many levels of sphagnum moss is no doubt well-preserved from the elements, dating from a time when the island was warmer and more densely populated.

The villages of the west side suffered worst during the Clearances, a legacy that rings in the phrase 'Mìorun Mór nan Gall' – 'the great ill will of the Lowlander' – and one I came to understand more deeply in the years to come, as I returned to Lewis to explore township after abandoned township.

On a bend in the river, Anne showed me the remains of Thulachan, five grass-covered mounds which were once part of a settlement. Slowly, the river had changed course and begun to erode the site, causing one of the mounds to collapse, spilling its contents into the fast-flowing water. Anne and I explored what was left, finding only charred wood, and then continued on our way, fording the brown, peat-coloured water.

Once across, the landscape stretched out with small undulations to the far hills, with every step across the peat made carefully. I was reminded by Anne that what appears as solid ground on the moor is often treacherous terrain. At one point, my walking pole slid effortlessly down into the bog, disappearing almost completely. The fear of a misplaced step into earth which could swallow me whole helped focus my mind and I followed Anne's barefoot steps intently. Other dangers included hidden river courses, holes and, of course, being exposed to the elements. Anne told me that on her last trip out, a lightning storm had made its way over the moor and, having known a good friend to have been struck while undertaking a similar expedition (the photographer Finn Ó Súilleabháin), my mind became intent on reaching shelter.

We had been walking and exploring now for the best part of an hour. With the weather closing in, wind and rain moving visibly toward us across the open moor, we took shelter and ate a quick snack in the ruins of a shieling with no roof. Sheltering against the high walls and waiting for the rain to pass, Anne commented that this type of easterly weather is known as a 'Red Wind' (Gaoth an ear-dheas – Dhearg) in Gaelic. As we listened to the low wind howling around us, I occupied myself by exploring the walls of the shieling, finding rusted pots and an old kettle amongst the long grass. With a break in the rain, we pushed on, at times following the footprints left by Anne from a previous journey made a week before, her tracks still perfectly preserved in the peat.

Passing a picturesque loch ringed by sundews, we stopped by the shieling once used by Anne's father before making our way onto the final hurdle, going over the top of Beinn Thùlagabhal. Having made it up the muddy flanks, we sat exhausted on the grassy top. Observing the wind and clouds moving quickly over the scene, I saw her family shieling for the first time. Thankfully, it was now close by and I couldn't wait to get there and find some shelter from the elements.

It wasn't long before we had skirted the edges of Loch nan Leac and were finally sitting inside the shieling, the wind howling relentlessly around us. Having come this far, we decided to erect an improvised roof over the shieling, something Anne had done many times before. Using nothing but plastic piping it wasn't long before she had created a rigid, skeleton-like frame, which we moved into position on the top of the structure. Standing a few metres above the ground, we teetered on the edge of the building as the wind blew us around, trying to anchor the ribs of the frame using rocks and the heaviest stones we could find. After several failed efforts we finally secured it, something which proved much easier than attaching the roof covering!

The wind caught the canvas roof like a sail, the material whipping around violently as we tried to anchor it. We both danced around the edge of the shieling trying to keep it down, the wind billowing up from the open doors below. After a long struggle – and collecting a few additional rocks – it was finally in place, yet threatened to blow off any time.

The rain was now driving hard and the wind getting stronger. Bran refused to come inside the shieling, as he was terrified by the horrendous noise made by the sheets flapping and cracking violently in the wind. It sounded as if a freight train was passing overhead and, although there was only a few feet between us, Anne and I had to shout our conversation to each other. Amidst the chaos of the storm, Anne lit a fire using dried peat and boiled water that she had collected from the loch. After two cups of warm Darjeeling tea, we reached the decision that staying out on the moor in this weather was probably not advisable.

While a quick meal cooked over the peat fire, filling the shieling with smoke, I examined the walls and noticed the carvings for the first time. The oldest – from 1821 – marked the date that the shieling was rebuilt from an earlier structure and another from 1921 commemorated this date. Anne was hopeful that she might add 2021 to the walls of the shieling, which were otherwise bare, save for a carving of a deer and the initials of those who had come before, including the much-loved Gaelic poet, Peter Campbell. Looking out through the open door facing out of the wind, I gazed out onto the moor while slowly starting to warm up. Time seemed briefly to have stopped.

With our meal over, we knew that there were only a few hours of light left and that if we didn't leave soon, we would be forced to walk across the land in darkness, a prospect that could prove dangerous. Still exhausted from our exertions, we packed the roofing materials away and began our long journey back. In my tiredness, I fell into a hollow, my body sinking into a hidden river, a caochan, up to my waist. Completely unexpected, it forced me to focus. Recovering quickly, we forded a succession of rivers and made our way towards the coastline and the village of Bragar beyond. In our tired state, we still managed to make good time.

The light turned from blue to grey to black and as we finally left the moor I had to make use of a torch to see the path in front of me, very thankful that I had Anne as a guide over the unfamiliar terrain. For days after I would be reminded of the journey, as the smell of peat smoke rose again from my belongings; but the memory of experiencing the moor in all weathers I will carry with me for years to come.

A few years would pass before I returned to Lewis and Harris, this time with my wife, Jessica. We were on the island to visit friends, to travel out to St Kilda where I was making images for a book, and to spend some time in Stornoway where I'd been offered an interview for a new role at An Lanntair Arts Centre as a curator and help/mentor working with artists from across the Outer Hebrides.

To my great shock, I was offered the job and it wasn't long before we'd moved our possessions to the village of Bragar, setting up our home in that same croft house from my first visit. We would spend two years on the island, experiencing its stunning summer mornings, with mist hanging above the mirror lochs, through to its harsh winters, where wind and driving rain force you round the fire and keep you indoors for months on end.

We slowly began to meet friends, mostly 'incomers' like ourselves who had moved to the Hebrides to experience a different way of living. We spent our time with people who had come from across the world to set up homes on Lewis and Harris and received such warmth and kindness during times of both happiness and hardship.

It is the collision of both old and new that makes the Isle of Rust so fascinating to outsiders such as myself and also provides many of the tensions for its inhabitants. It is undeniable that life on the island is changing. The gradual erosion of the influence of the Free Church of Scotland (and Free Church of Scotland Continuing) is accompanied by problems with an ever-ageing population and the greatest issue facing the Outer Hebrides today: that of depopulation, which is far above the UK average. Tourism helps to revitalise island life during the summer months but brings with it many problems, from overcrowded single track roads, to the shortage of housing brought on by second homes and holiday lets, depriving local people of places in which to raise their families.

While large parts of Lewis and Harris remain in private hands as sprawling sporting estates, thankfully communities are now taking back control, most notably in Galson in Lewis and the North and West Harris Trusts.

This book then is a collection of photographic sketches I made while living on Lewis, not as a touristic guide, more as a diary made over several years and seasons. It is a visual response to Jonathan's essay of the same name, which I often had in mind as I explored the themes of 'Isle of Rust' in mountains, moors and lochs.

Jonathan's writing has been highly influential on me throughout my life; his essay 'Death to the Picturesque' having been a particularly formative influence on my early photographic approach. I'm greatly honoured by the opportunity to include his work within this book and I have tried my best not to deviate from his direction to 'Emphasise the contrast between natural grandeur and scrap squalor'.

The Outer Hebrides have of course long attracted photographers. However, I have chosen not to follow in the footsteps of Paul Strand, Werner Kissling, Fay

Professor Murdo Macdonald HRSA, Stornoway, Lewis

Stacashal from the Pentland Road, Lewis

The mountains of North Harris

Ruined house on croft, Ballalan, Lewis

Godwin, Gus Wylie and Robert Moyes Adams, who captured the island in stark monochrome, opting instead for colour.

I took a truly Calvinistic approach to making images and limited myself to minimal equipment, in this case a camera and two lenses which I could carry across moors or up mountainsides. I photographed things as I found them. There are no attempts to create postcard images, no specialist filters, no long exposures of the incoming tide at Luskentyre, no misguided attempts to create anthropological studies of the islanders. There is only the available light, and the colours as my eyes experienced them. The beauty of the Hebridean landcape and light speak clearly enough without my interventions.

This approach does come with its own limitations, the most challenging of which is to communicate the endless changeability of light, the sheer variety of landscape and the complex, multifaceted nature of the place.

It would, as poet Norman MacCaig once said in 'By the Graveyard, Luskentyre', take a volume 'thick as the height of the Clisham' and 'big as the whole of Harris' to even begin to scratch the surface of gneiss, peat and lochan.

Hills of Lewis from Grabhair, Lewis

Isle of Rust

Jonathan Meades

THERE ARE OTHER Scotlands – vital, living, untarnished by Walter Scottishness. Places of the strangest energy and greatest delight.

Places that have no ancestral claim on us, where the yoke of a ready-made collective history is absent, which we can talk of in the future perfect rather than the past historic. Places that we can elect to go towards rather than come from. Places which are potential – where anything is possible, where everything is waiting to happen. Time for a rebirth…

There are places that we choose to attach ourselves to – or which choose us. Whose genius loci is so potent that it incites us to love them. The spirit of the place renders us incapable of resistance.

That spirit is not spiritual. It is, rather, a combination of geological, meteorological and man-made circumstances. It's the enveloping presence, the essence which incites sensations of transcendence, awe and bliss. These sensations do not depend on the exhortations and boasts of some intercessory deity, of a wrathful worm-god slithering through the eustachian tube to demand oblations for having worked to create this… this paradise.

This is the world's work of countless millions of years against which we measure ourselves and are found wanting. Passers-through and all that. A blink in the eye of eons.

Here, at the north-westernmost periphery of Europe is what feels like a presage of the future, the distant future, the furthest future, after which there'll be no future at all. This is the Isle of Rust – known, too, as Lewis and Harris. It is a blueprint, a working model of the day which will have no tomorrow.

It is an isle of countless mysteries, enduring mysteries.

The light is singular – constantly changing. The isle is porous – like petrified sponge. Its landscape is not landscape – it is liquid. Its waterscape is not waterscape – it is solid. There are areas of glacial erosion and of sedimentary transportation.

The metamorphic gneiss is 3,000 million years old. It is the result of several deformations. It is the oldest rock in Scotland – if this is Scotland, which I doubt. Obviously it is administratively Scotland but otherwise...

During the last ice age, the alternate pressures of freezing and thawing, expansion and contraction, combined with erosion to turn what had been monolithic into a moraine of millions of loose boulders. In Hindu mythology, similar rockscapes were formed by monkey gods – bad-tempered and, evidently, very strong brothers frenziedly hurling boulders at each other. Not here. There are no fratricidal monkey gods on the Isle of Rust.

Calvinistic Presbyterian mythology – which claims to be something other than mythology but isn't – decrees that God, the one God, created this Calvinistic Presbyterian island – boulders, lochs and all – in six days. Fair enough, we all know the lad's got a great engine on him – he's 100 per cent work-rate, a celestial Scholesy. But what if God's day is anyone else's couple of million years. What if his conception of clock-time and calendars does not correspond to the mundane artifices invented by emperors, popes and Swiss watchmakers?

On the seventh day he went down to the sea. He made water shimmering blue like his true love's eyes. He made sand fine and yellow as his true love's locks. He made machair so soft, his true love lay down to sleep forever.

Which may not have been part of the grand plan. No doubt he, too, hurled boulders in his wrathful grief. The quaint misattribution of this island's provenance, the denial of fact in favour of creation myth, should not bother us. The wonders of evolution are infinitely more subtle and fascinating than the coarse fabrications proposed by those repositories of ignorance called sacred texts – forgivable 2,000 years ago as a means of trying to understand our physical surroundings but inexcusable today.

Machair – pretty much peculiar to the Atlantic coast – is a work of millions of years of sand and crushed shells being blown and swept on to acidic peat. This creates a thin but exceptionally fertile soil which is further enriched by guano of ground-nesting birds – oystercatchers, sandpipers, terns, lapwings, redshanks, corncrakes, peewits – and by grazing cattle's dung. Does this mean that cattle are coprophagic? Let us dwell, rather, on orchids, clovers, daisies. And on the dunes between the sea and the machair where marram grass grows – a sort of armature, a set of reinforcing rods, that inhibits the shift of sand.

Peat occurs in exceptionally wet temperate or cold climates where vegetable matter, notably non-flowering plants such as sphagnum moss, is prevented from totally decomposing by an excess of water. Certain species of sphagnum have spore

Cloud on the Clisham horseshoe, Harris

Red deergrass on the Clisham (An Clisham) with Toddun in the distance, Harris

Dun Carloway, Carloway, Lewis

Butterfly caught on the Barvas moor, Lewis

capsules which shrink to the point where the air within them is so compressed that they explode – noisily. This may partially account for the belief – the literal belief – that peat moors are inhabited by boisterous bog sprites who infect so much twilit Celtic folklore.

Peat used to roast barley famously lends the whisky made from that malt an operating theatre bouquet. When taken in sufficient quantity, that liquor can doubtless convince the most obdurately rational mind that green creatures dance by night on the desolate moors. These creatures – some amiable, some malevolent, some the spirits of the dead, some fallen from heaven – were thought to inhabit unseen places beneath the earth and under pools which would be revealed as the world ended. Peat is dug and dried for slow-burning fuel. It is host to many heathers.

Because of a lack of oxygen and an abundance of acids, it preserves animal bodies and human bodies – the bodies of those who have stumbled into its bogs and those who have been murdered or ritually executed. Almost 2,000 bodies have so far been discovered in such diverse places as South Uist, Cheshire, Jutland, Varberg in Sweden, County Meath, Groningen in the northern Netherlands. But none has been found yet far on the Isle of Rust. The likely reason for this is that the topography is inimical to the industrialised peat cutting which has revealed most of the bodies so far. But we can go on hoping. The ligature or noose will often be preserved too. The process is closer to pickling than to mummification. And it is rapid. Though most of the bog bodies that have been discovered are more than 1,000 years old, a Second World War soldier has been exhumed in a perfect state of preservation.

These bogs are full of future potential. It is not inconceivable that devices which can detect the limbs of the dead beneath metres of peat are in an advanced state of development. So we can meet our ancestors by design rather than by the chance of a plough or harrow. And if we cannot meet them in the flesh, we can at least meet them in the leather. It beats reading a name on a birth certificate.

There are golden eagles in the mountains. Soaring no doubt. And buzzards drifting on thermals looking to transform a harmless mammal into lunch. White-tailed sea eagles – whose wingspan is over eight feet (two and a half metres) – patrol the coast. They live on fish with carrion on the side. There is little competition for prey with golden eagles who eat rabbit, hare, grouse – which makes them unpopular with gamekeepers and hunters.

There are ospreys; hen harriers which are white-bellied buzzards; peregrine falcons; kestrels; shags; and fulmars who can eject an oil reeking of putrefying fish from their stomach to fend off attackers. This oil swiftly solidifies to a sort of wax which can be incapacitating. Beside them, hoodie crows who merely pluck out the eyes of lambs seem paragons of moderation. It should be noted that all of these species are recidivist sociopaths, murderous delinquents even into their maturity – they are thus bad role models for youngsters. They may inhabit paradise but they make it hell for their prey.

There are deer everywhere. They don't fly – save in France, where a kite is called a flying stag, *un cerf volant*. There are hare; rabbits; otters; bottle-nosed dolphins; seals; basking sharks that are allegedly harmless though it's hardly worth the risk of finding out; brown trout – the ones with the white flesh which taste so much better than gaudy rainbow trout; salmon; and cannibalistic crustaceans.

There are slow worms – which are legless lizards – but no snakes. So despite the ancient belief that Barvas Moor was the Garden of Eden, it obviously wasn't. Unless, that is, the snake – as maligned as Judas but as necessary to the story's structure – moved on once it had performed its role. No doubt some of the many other claimants to Edenhood – the source of the Tigris, a spring in Jerusalem and so on – are more climatically plausible and, of course, they are in the Middle East, font of all monotheistic mumbo-jumbo. But are any of them as primal, as

primitive, as truly paradisiac as this elemental moor whose Gaelic name is Barabhas – like that of the outlaw or terrorist whom the mob had necessarily to wish pardoned in order that it be Jesus who died.

It is more Calvary than Eden. Abattoir rather than cradle.

This is the northwestern extremity of Europe. It prompts wonder. It prompted wonder and bewilderment to our distant, preliterate forebears. And it prompted, too, the urge to investigate and measure what was around them.

They had no recourse to the supernatural. They calibrated their place in their surroundings by marking the actual: where the sun sets at the vernal equinox; where it rises at the summer solstice; the positions of constellations, the vagaries of the moon.

This was practical. This was the first germ of what would become science. Curiosity sated by investigation rather than by crude hypotheses. These sites may have been calendars of a sort. Unlike the much more extensive menhirs at Carnac in southern Brittany, it's improbable that they were instruments to foretell earth tremors – no area of Britain is less susceptible to seismic activity. It's likely that they were also places of celebration – of the sun which provided power and warmth, greater warmth 5,000 years ago than it provides here today; of the moon which determined tides and illumined the interminable winter nights. Celebration isn't the same as worship. The presence of ritual – which appeals to a certain cast of mind with a fondness for occluded drama and ancient conspiracies – cannot be confirmed. Nor for that matter denied, though it is worth noting that, while these stones are 5,000 years old, Wicca, Druidism and Paganism are little more than 300 years old and much ancient ritual derives from polytechnics in the 1970s and '80s.

It was about that time, too, that Celtic folk rock established itself here and in Brittany, Ireland and Galicia – a cleverly marketed kind of pop music based on nationalistic sentimentalism, on a sense of victimhood, on the Celtic world's secessionist destiny and on an antipathy to the primacy of the English, French and Castilian languages. The entire package is as rooted in historical certainty as tartan and Ossian's epic. Which doesn't mean that it is not real. Bogusness has its own reality. The nature of these sites' funerary roles and their uses as commemorative cemeteries is moot.

But the disposition of boulders by evolution is visually random. We obviously witness it on this island. We see it, too, on the Breton coast near Carnac and in the sarsens on the Marlborough Downs near Avebury – sarsens that were often mistaken for sheep. Which must have caused some embarrassing injuries. The presumption that henges and menhirs and dolmens are sacred is based more in the interpretative and speculative biases of the early modern age which first concerned itself with such phenomena than in irrefutable evidence.

The ascription of fancifully conceived primitive belief systems to our ancestors is wrongheaded. The contention that the religious instinct was paramount in all peoples and in all epochs is taken for granted, which is a good reason to question it. Why should ancient man have been any different from us? Some of us are credulous, more are not. In societies where there is no cultural coercion or political obligation, we believe or don't believe according to our conscience and intellect. It is patronising and ahistorical to assume – as Neo-Celtic musicians appear to – that the ancient Gaelic world was monocultural. Some sites may have been sacred, others secular.

What is indisputable about these sites is that they tell us mankind is a maker. That is what is paramount. They do not tell us why they were made. And we shall never know for sure. Given a few pebbles and an idle moment, many of us will position them in lines, grade them according to size, form elementary shapes with them. This could very likely be diagnosed as symptomatic of obsessive compulsive disorder. Which it was not called all those millennia ago. Mankind obsessively devises patterns. Maybe these sites have no meaning. They are patterns made for their own sake or for the sake of controlling their environment.

Maybe they are pre-Euclidean exercises in creating a non-representational kind of art, specifically what we know as land art. An art based in the collection and regimentation of local materials which happen, in the case of gneiss or granite, to be durable. There may have been thousands of kindred sites constructed in areas of friable material – chalk or sandstone or gritstone or wood. Sites which have not come down to us because they rapidly eroded or rotted leaving no trace. Our knowledge is dependent on geological chance.

The most circumstantially persuasive argument for these Neolithic sites being sacred rather than the result of collective OCD is their very location. Which is topographically and climatically extreme.

It is in such exaggerated places that religions are born and it's where they flourish: deserts, steppes, tundra, mountains, salt flats, aridity, permafrost – these are propitious conditions for the shift into hallucinatory unreason that is dignified by the name of faith. The more extreme a landscape or climate, the greater its effects on its inhabitants.

Temperate climes are, happily, less effective cradles of what David Hume called 'sick men's dreams'. They promote the greatest of human virtues, cynicism – in its true sense. The UK, France and Denmark are the least observant countries in western Europe. For the moment.

The Isle of Rust is entirely atypical of the UK as it is today. There are 50 churches – one for every 400 people – in a population of 22,000. Over a third of those people attend a church every Sunday. A vastly larger proportion than anywhere else in Britain. Though it must be noted, too, that two thirds of the population are not observant. The church at Rodel, founded by a gentleman called Hunchbacked Alasdair, is the most impressive medieval building on Rust. But it would be nothing special elsewhere in north Britain. It is the exception that proves the rule of the island's churches' unfailing banality.

And unfailing dreariness. The idea that a church might be visually enjoyable is alien to Calvinism. Enjoyment?! Indeed, while Presbyterian sects are forever diverging over doctrinal nuances invisible to the lay observer, they are united in their contempt for the pursuit of beauty. The jezebel called architecture is a papist strumpet. Icons are sacrilegious. Music is the devil's work. Ritual is theatre – which is an abomination. To delight the eye is an offence against modesty. These paltry insipid buildings are slights to mankind: they are incitements to lead a life in fear of life. They are the very obverse of the great

Macleod's standing stone, Isle of Harris

View to Luskentyre and the mountains of Harris, Seilebost, Harris

Back Free Church, Lewis

stone circles which are hymns to mankind.

Unlike Anglicanism, Calvinism demands commitment. It is a matter of conviction and unconditional acquiescence. It affects the way its adherents lead their constrained life. Even though it is today a minority pathology – just – it still attempts to create a cultural tyranny and to impose its morals and wacky brand of tolerance on the majority – who can think for itself.

The most evident manifestation of the sacred's contamination of the secular is on Sundays. The Lord's day. The Sabbath. Even though, despite the clamorous minority's objections, a Sunday ferry now sails, the island closes down. The majority of the vehicles to be seen are those of church-goers. Work of any sort is disapproved of but so is leisure – don't tend your garden, don't go for a walk, don't listen to music, don't go fishing, don't swim. Don't… don't… don't… Proscribe this. Prohibit that.

The cause may be delusional credulousness – but it results in the greatest of modern luxuries. Silence. Calm. Something close to serenity. It causes us to realise that there is a secular case for Sabbatarianism. For, anyway, a day that is different – not necessarily Sunday – a day when there is nowhere to lout about at lunchtime, to chant in the afternoon, to get into a stramash, to buy pointless things in an atmosphere where your ears hurt because of drivelling pop-noise and your nose hurts because of burger stench. It is, of course, conceivable that the Sabbath is uncomplainingly observed because much of the population is in no condition to do anything but slump after the previous evening's Nordic exertions.

Our race's most widespread means of escapism are religious faith and insensate intoxication. For a totally satisfactory result combine the two in the manner of dervishes, berserkers, shamans.

Oh! They certainly know how to escape themselves. A kip in the pews and a copious supply of Irn-Bru is just the ticket after a gallon of heavy plus chasers.

Until the beginning of this decade, all alcohol was imported.

In 2000, Marco Tayburn set up the Abhainn Dhearg Distillery (The Red River Distillery) and the year after Andrew Ribbens established the Hebridean Brewery. Apt if belated, for whisky is the only Gaelic word most of the world knows and this island has Scotland's largest concentration of Gaelic speakers.

If, that is, one discounts Glasgow's Gaelic-speaking ghetto of: Gaelic language media dimensioning operatives; Gaelic language propagation strategists; Gaelic language participation leaders; Gaelic language education vanguard light managers; Gaelic language ambit teachers' teachers;

Gaelic language vision lobbyists; Gaelic language sit-on-my-face-book inscribers; Gaelic language horizontal sausaging matrix implementers; Gaelic language translatability facilitators; Gaelic language fellation development officers; Gaelic language signage advisors and Gaelic language supremacists.

The self-important sociolinguistic industry is, of course, risible but the language it supports most certainly isn't. That only 60,000 people speak it is no reason to allow it to wither on the tongue. The fact that it might be more practical to allow the English language to vanquish it is of no moment. Practicality is an infirm criterion. Think of Gaelic as a threatened system of cultural ecology or compare it to a species nearing extinction or a spirituous liquor which might disappear because the recipe was lost. As in a way it was. There is, of course, a generalised Gaelic culture as bogus as the plaid and pipes of the Highlands – bardic and bearded with a brand of folk rock and a typeface that links Galicia, Brittany, western Ireland and the Hebrides in a cisatlantic union of minoritarian defiance.

But there is much that is peculiar to Rust. Guga, for instance. Gannets. Ten men make the hazardous 40-mile journey each August to the uninhabited island of Sula Sgeir. They spend a fortnight trapping and salting around 2,000 chicks. This was once alimentary necessity. The meat apparently tastes like chicken fed on fish meal. I shall give it a miss, like I gave fermented trout a miss.

I wish I'd given whale a miss. But I was only three – at a picnic on a Dorset beach. It would have been discourteous to refuse the lumps of grey gelatinous meat beneath an undercooked pastry crust. It was like chewing an eraser.

On Harris, a whaling station was operational from 1904 till a few years after the Second World War. Whales were processed for ambergris, a constituent of perfumes; for oil and wax, which were used in soap and candles; and margarine, which explains a lot. The meat – cheap, plentiful, unpleasant – was a staple part of islanders' diet.

A lot of food is still produced here. But much of it is beyond the inhabitants' means – scallops, lobster, crayfish and so on. But not salmon which is so intensively farmed that its price has plummeted along with its quality.

The lochs are factories. And like factories they manifest what might be called an industrial style – though that's pushing it a bit. Sub-utilitarian is more like it. Herrings and salmon are kippered, salmon is cold smoked and cured as gravlax.

Macleod and Macleod, Charles Macleod, WJ Macdonald, A. and R. Morrison, A. France. All of these butchers make the best, the truly original, the most authentic Stornoway marag dhubh (black pudding). It is the peer of the best Blutwurst, boudin noir and morcilla. It can sit at the top table and hold its own.

Highland cattle. Crowdie cheese. Beef. Sheep. Lamb. Hogget. Wether. Tweed.

A toy fortress was built by Sir James Matheson in 1848. It's in a style that a plutocrat might have chosen 25 years earlier, long before Victoria's accession. Which is not surprising because Matheson had been out east for all that time. He was a trader, that is to say a drug dealer – on a heroic scale that the Medellin cartel can only look on with envious wonder. This god-fearing teetotaler bought the entire isle with a fortune made from transporting opium from India to China and from promoting addictive dependence in tens of thousands of people in southern China.

It was on behalf of Matheson and his fellow dealers when they were expelled by the Chinese government that Britain waged the ignominious opium wars. Matheson should have been imprisoned. Instead he received a baronetcy and, like many criminals before and since, became a member of Parliament whereupon he proposed that the grim lump of rock called North Rona, 60 kilometres north of here, should be turned into a high-security jail. He built his castle on the site of the isle's only distillery – thus encouraging the use of illicit stills.

While the castle is, despite its size, rather trivial, the remarkable grounds lead us to understand that zoos and aviaries and parks and arboreta – despite their association with the Enlightenment's propagation of knowledge – were founded by men trying to play at God. Trying to mimic what was still widely considered to be his creation. They belong, sentimentally, to an age before reason. Or at least to an age before humility and reason told man that he was no more capable of controlling the world than a god had been of having created it.

In Matheson's native Northern Highlands, the Clearances of crofters had been undertaken by landowners and clans chiefs in what they believed – or at least deluded themselves – was a spirit of philanthropic noblesse oblige. The so-called improvements were as much a project of Enlightenment pedagogy as of agrarian capitalism.

People who could barely read or write and who subsisted in insanitary bothies, burrows and caves were forcibly removed from the land – the land which hardly yielded them a living.

Some were provided with houses, jobs and education in the new grid-plan fisher-towns of the Sutherland and Caithness coasts, some were transported across the Atlantic. The moors they had inhabited were made over to sheep. By the mid-19th century, all philanthropic pretence had been abandoned. Matheson proceeded to treat the islanders

– his islanders – with the same sensitivity that he had displayed in Canton, though they were not provided with the balmy solace of narcosis. He did not build a fisher-town. In the early years of the 1850s, almost 2,000 inhabitants were forcibly expatriated, mostly to Canada, their passage paid by Matheson. The suppression of whisky was calculated. The suppression of Gaelic was a clumsy consequence of the involuntary diaspora.

What Matheson did build was roads – they provided work during the famine years of the 1840s. He intended that they should be used to transport peat so that it might be transformed into tar: the scheme was a nonstarter. On the mainland, such roads came to be known as destitution roads because they were built by the destitute and it was along them that the indigent marched away from destitution to their uncertain future on the other side of the world. The name is prescient. Today they still often lead to destitution.

Whatever wealth is generated is mostly well-concealed. It is very seldom manifest in the built environment. There are some works of architectural merit on the isle. Well, two. And they seem impertinently pretentious measured against the startlingly abject norm.

This is perhaps the only place in the world whose townships and villagescapes, urbanism and landscapes are wholly infected by the Calvinist mentality – that is, by a blindness to prettification, an ignorance of any recognisable notion of beauty, by an aesthetic bereavement so absolute that it is a sort of insouciant anti-aesthetic. In a way, the everyday buildings are the very contrary of Matheson's. They suggest that to compete with this most magnificent terrain would be both hubristic and certain failure. So they simply didn't bother to compete. The unsurpassable strangeness of the isle resides in the chasmic gulf between the naturally evolved and the negligently created, between scarp and scrap, between the sublime and the substandard.

Not that the natural is invariably natural: it generally isn't. The landscape most formed by man here is not that of menhirs and dolmens. In fact, man is moot in this context. The cable-knitted hillsides are the work of the sheep that man introduced. They sit alongside the field systems called run rig or lazy beds. This corrugated pattern of drainage furrows – the runs – and of fertile ridges – the rigs – is mostly in desuetude. But it is so widespread that it is one of the defining characteristics of the landscape. These systems, like stone circles, possess a kind of abstract integrity that often attaches to the purely practical.

The steadings and smallholdings, too, are purely practical. But where the field systems are ordered, the buildings are extraordinarily chaotic.

Shepherdess on the Pentland Road, Lewis

Ruined house, Isle of Scalpay

Rig and furrow field systems, Harris

Former scout hut, Harris

The isle's shackscape is the apogee of the northern Hebridean anti-aesthetic.

Members of the National Trust and kindred bastions of insipid taste will doubtless fail to recognise the fantastical beauty of what is here – they should be pitied and soothed with a Glamis tea towel.

These scapes are beautiful in the way that a lupus is beautiful, or mould on fruit, or decaying meat, or scar tissue, or amputations, or diseases of the skin, or anatomical freaks. They exert the same pull.

This is the great outdoors as it might have been conceived by hothouse poets of the darkest indoors, by virtuosi of polymorphous perversion: Francis Bacon and Arthur Tress, Joel-Peter Witkin and Félicien Rops.

It's everything that planning can never achieve. Art born of artlessness and carelessness – as though man has hurled temporary structures like the old gods hurled boulders.

It is a thrilling environment made by a beguiling lack of respect for that most sacred of cows, 'the environment' – worthy, green, dull and tiresomely backward-looking. Put a petrol head in a pedestrian precinct and you'll get a fascinating crash.

And once the entropic template was established, it was repeated with endless amendments and in countless permutations.

There is nothing that cannot be used as an ad-hoc folly, as a felicity beacon, as an iconic icon. And there is apparently no one on the isle who is immune to the appeal of the found object and the oxidising object.

Whoever would have thought that the last remaining bastion of fundamentalist Calvinism would become the site of a scrap cult. That the most seductive collective expression of Gaelic vernacular culture would involve immobile bulldozers, holed boats, Allegros buried in dunes.

Whoever would have thought…

We should think again. This isle nation, this rather enchanted isle is a law unto itself. De jure it belongs to Scotland. De facto it belongs to itself – it's a tartan-free zone.

Far from being stuck in the Scottish past, it presages the not very distant future when continents and nations and regions and towns and villages split into ever-smaller fragments according to their language, their patois, their schismatic religion, their wacko culture – and their peripherality.

Other extremities of this continent spell out their situation: Finistera, Finisterre, Land's End. Rust may stay schtumm about it but this is the end of the world – the old world – and the beginning of a new one.

It does indeed foster a minority culture which has the strength of its self-consciousness. Its language is a means of communication but it is equally a cause spoken by very few people. It is abnormally religiously observant. Other nations and nation states will catch up. It will come to seem normal. There can, regrettably, be little doubt that this century will witness a religious revival like that of the second quarter of the 19th century.

It suffers exemplary conditions to succour the 21st century's gradual isolation and subsequent atomisation. This is the Wi-Fi wilderness – when the Wi-Fi is not climatically disrupted. Like poor crofters and weavers before them, its inhabitants are discovering the hell that is home-working. Offices, labs, studios, canteens are social places. There are no canteens in the wilderness. There are no snout-casts gathered outside a door shivering into their gaspers.

How long before we succumb to the woolly temptresses on the moor who shamelessly go naked even on the Sabbath? How long can we survive being trapped in a virtual cage? That is a bit of a mystery. There are, however, much greater mysteries to dwell on.

How do you get a Ford Transit into the middle of a peat bog?

I'm not expecting an answer to that. Nor to the question of how you get a Mini Metro into the middle of a peat bog and then turn it upside-down?

These vehicles will gradually be enveloped by sphagnum moss. Several millennia hence, in a world ignorant of internal combustion, they will be discovered in a state of at least partial preservation and revered as sacred objects from a distant, pre-apocalyptic age – a paradisiac age which ended with a bleat and a rusted carburettor.

Transit van on moorland, Lemreway, Lewis

ISLE OF RUST

A VISUAL JOURNEY

AROUND

LEWIS & HARRIS

Bog cotton, Shawbost, Lewis

Ruin and caravan, Callanish, Lewis

Ship's boiler, Gress, Lewis

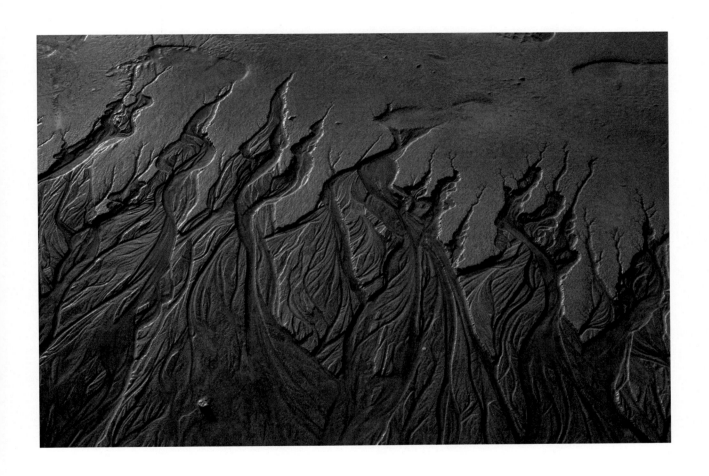

Sand after the tide, Vatisker, Lewis

Cottage on Bhaltos peninsula, Lewis

Bus repurposed as shieling, Cuishader, Lewis

Former tweed mill, Newmarket, Lewis

Wetlands, Harris

Abandoned cut peats, Bragar, Lewis

New shieling, Cuishader, Ness, Lewis

Car wrecks, Great Bernara

Cut peats, North Tolsta, Lewis

Caves near Vatisker, Lewis

Former Ministry of Defence buildings, Aird Uig, Lewis

David and Paula Brown, Shawbost, Lewis

Old school, Brenish, Lewis

Sron Ulladale, highest cliff-face in the UK, Harris

Ruined van, Achmore, Lewis

Abandoned cottage near Maraig, Harris

Ruined cottage, Bays of Harris, Harris

Bus stop with religious graffiti, Back, Lewis

Ruined bus, Back, Lewis

Bus repurposed as store, Brue, Lewis

Abandoned bus, North Tolsta, Lewis

Dalmore beach and graveyard, Lewis

Abandoned bus, Brue, Lewis

Abandoned trailer park, Back, Lewis

The wild ponies of Luskentyre, Harris (R)

Shieling, Cuishader, Lewis

Harbour, Isle of Scalpay

Shed near Lemreway, Lewis

Tennis court, Harris

Peat cuttings, Harris

Callanish standing stones, Lewis

Gun emplacements, Arnish point, Lewis

Big Blue Party Bus (former), Point, Lewis

Renovated cottage, Borve, Harris

Lamb and mother, Isle of Scalpay

Upturned car, Flesherin, Lewis

Storm approaching the Valtos peninsula, Lewis

Ruins at the mouth of the Creed, Stornoway Castle grounds, Lewis

Jessica Danz, composer, Back, Lewis

Abandoned Land Rover, Lower Bayble, Lewis

Bus stop and office chair, Kendebig, Harris

Barrels in the hold of the *Creteree*, concrete ship, Isle of Scalpay

The First World War concrete ship *Cretetree*, Isle of Scalpay

Bus repurposed for storage, North Tolsta, Lewis

Second World War Stornoway Harbour defences, Arnish, Lewis

Interior of ruined cottage, Bays of Harris

Cuishader village paths,
Ness, Lewis

Sheep, Loch Seaforth,
Harris

Bins and ruined cottage, Callanish

End of the road, Hushinish,
Harris

Croft, Bunabhainneader, Harris

Wetlands, Harris

The Clisham,
Harris

Modern shieling, moorland, Lewis

Second World War observation station, Aird, Lewis

Blowhole in sea cave, Shawbost, Lewis

Telegraph pole, Isle of Scalpay

Hay bales, Vatisker, Lewis

Caravan with ruin, Achmore, Lewis

Hills near Uig, Lewis

Ruined cottage near
Rhenigidale, Lewis

Coastal road,
Harris

View to Toddun, Rhenigidale, Harris

Road to Uig, Lewis

Carloway Free
Church, Lewis

Blue barrels from the fishing boat *Serene*, Isle of Bernera

Ship's boilers, Isle of Scalpay

Mountains, Harris

Deerstalker's path to Sron Ulladale, Harris

Road to Uig, Lewis

Ruined cars, near Amhuinnsuidhe Castle, Isle of Harris

Boulders on Ben Bragar,
Shawbost, Lewis

Detail from wreck of fishing boat *Genesis*, Kirkibost, Great Bernera

Reliant Robin, Stornoway

Kevin Wrigglesworth, engineer, Back, Lewis (L) Dr Louise Senior, Harris (R)

View to South Lochs from Ballalan, Lewis

Atlantic waves,
Hushinish, Harris

Road to the beach, Vatisker, Lewis

Unidentified object, Achmore, Lewis

Andy Laffan, sculptor, Lewis (L) Ship's propeller, Goat Island, Lewis (R)

Ships under repair, Goat Island yard, Lewis

Abandoned cottage near Callanish, Lewis

Disused phone box, near Griomarstaidh, Lewis

Car wreck, moorland near Newmarket, Lewis

Gus's Mobile Shop (no longer mobile), Leverburgh, Harris

Former military building, Aird Uig, Lewis

Rusted bicycle, Bragar, Lewis

Rusting weaving equipment, Gress, Lewis

The Atlantic,
Hushinish, Harris

The road to Hushinish, Harris

The summit cairn of Ben Bragar, Lewis

Vatisker and Back Free Church, Lewis

Road to Ben Bragar, Shawbost, Lewis

Industrial shed, Baile an Truiseil, Lewis

Fishing boat, Callanish, Lewis

Paul, Gemma and Emily, Croft 2B,
North Tolsta, Lewis

Former whaling station, Harris

The dunes of Luskentyre beach, Harris

Former trailer park, Back, Lewis

Car wreck, Shawbost, Lewis

Abandoned cottages, Balallan, Lewis

Bus stop, Vatisker, Lewis

Port Stoth, near Butt of Lewis, Lewis

Wreck of fishing boat, Goat Island, Lewis

Scrapyard, Ness, Lewis

Sea near Bayble, Lewis

Rusting work van, Point, Lewis

Andrea Ingram, photographer (L) and her wife, Evelyn Dunstan, professional cyclist (R)

Religious Book Shop (former), Stornoway

Restored house, Shawbost, Lewis

Path to Luskentyre Beach, Harris

Cleared village, Mealasta, Lewis

Abandoned whaling factory, Harris

Wrecked vehicles, Great Bernera

Ruin, Isle of Scalpay

Ruined cottage, Isle of Scalpay

Callanish standing stones and chambered cairn, Lewis

Gleann Mhiabhaig and Sron Scourst, Harris

Rusted car parts, Bragar, Lewis

Callanish standing stones, Lewis

Red cottage, Hushinish, Harris

Event Density

Dan Hicks

'IMMOBILE BULLDOZERS, HOLED boats, Allegros buried in the dunes.' The cadaver of a Ford Transit that is sinking into the bog. The ridge and furrow of land drainage. A shackscape of corrugated iron and raw timber. The towers and turrets of James Matheson's castellated mansion. The 'unspiritual' spirit of the Callanish Standing Stones, a Neolithic monument cut from the peat in 1857. The thought of undiscovered prehistoric bodies with ligatures perfectly preserved round the neck by the anaerobic acidity of the land itself.

Just what kind of archaeology is it that runs through Jonathan Meades' essay on Lewis and Harris and Rust? And how should we understand its affinity with the sheer humanity of Alex Boyd's photographs? Three suggestions.

First, maybe both involve some genre of *visual archaeology*. The text and the images share a way of looking. It somehow flips the backward vision with which self-consciously academic writing about the human past so often fixes itself; it does not bury its head in its hands to visualise a world gone by but transforms the present before our eyes. Excavation.

Discovery. Appearance. We're a long way from those three most deadening words in academic discourse – *critical, heritage, studies*. Could we even be beyond the influence of that very English prejudice towards honouring, preserving and curating those failed mid-1980s attempts by historians to co-opt the perspectives of Social Anthropology? It was a putsch driven by little more than shoring up against the threat of francophone deconstruction, the desire to set some parameters to the new relativism; a reduction of our understanding of the past to mere artifice and say-so. Social construction. Contextual interpretation. *The Invention of Tradition.*

It was Eric Hobsbawm and Terry Ranger's names on the book spine that bore that title when it hit the library shelves in 1983. It was, however, neither the Marxist nor the Africanist who contributed the text's ur-example but rather the Borderer, Hugh Trevor-Roper, whose snooty critique of Scottish nationalism re-described the very notion of Highland and Islands culture as nothing but a modern fabrication of bagpipe tartanry misrepresented as ancient custom.[1] Not for nothing did Neal Ascherton call him 'the Liquidator'.[2] It's still too close in intellectual history for us yet to have found a name for the Tory po-mo for which the operation of HT-R's deconstructionist falsifications of belief, of identity, of the work of culture, formed a central motor. But what is clear is that it revealed within the anthropologist's so-called reflexivity a kind of self-regard. As the Liquidator-General himself put it in his valedictory lecture on leaving Christ Church, Oxford to become Master of Peterhouse, Cambridge in 1980, the claim was that, 'Objective science has its place in historical study, but it is a subordinate place: the heart of the subject is not in the method but in the motor, not in the technique but in the historian'.[3] It was surely no coincidence that Trevor-Roper's laissez-faire snobbery towards those duped by *The Invention of Tradition* was published within just a few weeks of his authentication of the bogus Hitler Diaries.

The parallel visions of Meades-Boyd on Lewis-Harris operate against the 1980s Trevor-Roperian liquidations that still, inexplicably, hold so much currency in 'critical' 'heritage' circles; they lift our view of the past beyond an introspective mode, decentre the donnish sneer at plain invention, understand the vernacular past as something more than mere fanaticism, don't sniff at the composition of the past. They open their eyes to the humanity that inheres in what outlasts people's lives.

Second, then, there is in Meades-Boyd some kind of shared attention to *the detritus of human life*; it is an attitude that is geographical as well as temporal. Lewis and Harris is remote, at one end of an Antillean-like island chain, and yet somehow two islands in one, the Outer-Hebridean Haiti-Dominican Republic. Never mind 'invented traditions': this is a place not of false consciousness but double-consciousness, not of fake invention but transformation and multiplication.

The anthropologist Edwin Ardener began a list of the characteristics of remoteness, an unfinished list that included: '*Remote areas are full of innovators*'. '*Remote areas are in constant contact with the world*'. '*Remote areas are full of ruins of the past*'. '*Remote areas are full of rubbish*'. For Ardener there were connections between these axioms and paradoxes. He was talking about the Western Isles. It was the mid-1980s, again. Ardener reproduced a contemporary description by the journalist Derek Cooper of some objects around a crofthouse in Lewis:

Five hundredweight van (circa 1950s); Ford tractor minus one wheel; fragment of pre-Great War reaper; upright piano; 37 blue plastic fishboxes; 7 green lemonade crates; 2 chimney pots; a sizeable pyramid of sand; a pile of cement blocks; 7 lobster creels; assorted timber; 2 bales of barbed wire (rusted); broken garden seat; Hercules bicycle frame; piece of unidentified machinery (loom?); a sofa.[4]

There had been, Cooper suggested, less rubbish here in the 19th century. Sooty thatch was used as fertiliser. Fishing boats were recycled as roof timbers or furniture. Ropes made of heather and hemp would degrade. Flour sacks were sewn up as children's clothes. 'Then came the Galvanised Iron Age, the Brass Bedstead Age and the Plastics Age,' Cooper wrote; indestructible products of the industrial and consumer society; materials that are impossible to dispose of like fibreglass, plastic, aluminium, rubber; the accelerating obsolescence of accelerating imports.

It'd be easy to mistake these landscapes for ruins. A new generation of Liquidators is filling the pages of the 'critical' 'heritage' journals with newly insouciant and flaneuristic forms of self-regard: ruin porn, dereliction tourism, Anthropocenes, Chthulucenes, object-oriented ontologies of new vibrant nonhuman materialities, posthuman futurities, capitalist realisms. The full constructivist actor-network from HT-R to A-NT. Symmetrical archaeographies. Speculative nihilisms. Sustained manglings of Benjaminian aura in the face of duration, FFS.

Rust is not ruin. Here, the question of rubbish is a question of the visibility of decay, which is to say it is a question of geography. Commodity chains are one-way streets. At the end of the line things seem to pile up. There is of course far less waste in any remote place, it's just far more visible than in the metropolis. The course of obsolescence is less certain since innovation operates at a different pace, refracted through accumulation and repurposing, improvisation and human life. This is how in remote places the double-consciousness of place starts to give way to a double-consciousness of time. Provisionality gains a kind of depth. Events, Ardener tells us, have a more solid quality. The stuff that happens 'matters' more. There is a different event density.

Third, something about *a remoteness of time*, as well as just a remoteness of place, is shared in the visions of Meades and Boyd. We don't have to believe that the ineffable gneisses of Callanish were arranged as some kind of astronomical calendar that measured the movement of the moon against the horizon in order to affirm that this remote monument serves to measure the passing of time. They embody the ongoing density of events in this landscape; the environment itself calibrates minutes and months and years with rock and machair and sheep; Cambrian, Silurian, Quaternary, this is a place of remote innovation rather than retrospective invention; a folded landscape of unfolding events.

It can't be quite right that the passage from

Neolithic to Modern runs from Richard Long to Arthur Tress. There is a mutual directionality in the monumental and the transformational. Maybe it's something like Robert Smithson's lecture on Hotel Palenque, read in 1972 to the architectural faculty at the University of Utah. When Smithson visited this ramshackle Mexican hotel, it was undergoing a process of renovation that simultaneously involved the dismantling of some of its wings alongside the construction of others; he identified a spirit of simultaneous renovation and decay in the ancient Mayan ruins as well as in that dilapidated contemporary building. The image is one of a de-architecture of decay and potential that is ripping stuff down and building it up in a single gesture and is thereby bringing about not so much an architectural form as a form of comparison. An environment in which one remote place or time can come to stand for another that it does not resemble.[5] A place for thinking through looking. A Victorian Neolithic. An aluminium geology. The persistent physicality of loss.

Or maybe another lecture, John Ruskin's 'The World of Iron in Nature, Art and Policy' given at Tunbridge Wells in February 1858, where he denied that rusty iron is spoiled iron, since 'iron rusted is living; but when pure or polished, dead'. While gold and silver, which do not rust, have surely only brought bloody violence and death in the human past, by inhaling oxygen this metal – ferrous, magnetic, transitional – can become somehow 'nobler' with each flushed, corrosive gasp. Ruskin called up images of a horror-filled world where meadows grow not grass but iron wire, and arable land is reduced to flat surfaces of steel: images that he contrasted with that intake of breath through which the atmosphere can colour the world to make the sand yellow and the brick and tile red. In Lewis and Harris the flush of the brine in the wind brings these colours even to galvanised steel.

These are places for comparison, perhaps that is what we are learning here; places of analogy: as with Smithson's anti-ruin, as with Ruskin's anti-rust, so with Meades and Boyd and the scrap-cult of standing stones and Ford Transits. There's more at stake than just reading human life as if it were natural history, which would after all simply read Ruskinian pathetic fallacy back-to-front. No, there are gaps and absences here that hold the same event density, negative traces of evictions and abandonments, negative traces left from the grand Malthusian experiment of the Clearances, not just a failed innovation but one that commanded a linear, progressive, artificial vision of time, enacted that vision. Something akin to tradition works against such horror, against the force in which the picturesque itself was complicit (a way of seeing without transforming giving way to a contemplative past, the barbaric pretence of island 'savages' by a drug-dealing imperialist, and transportation far beyond this most remote of places).

Against such violence experiences of belonging and of community could never be false consciousness or mere invention. They emerge though the double consciousness of memory in a remote place where the density of events can be felt more clearly than the age of its monuments can be measured. Did the ideology of progressive time emerge in the metropolis because of the illusion that every road in the known world might lead to the library's door? If so then the counterpoint may be that in the Isle of Rust a sense of accumulated time is an effect of geographical distance, of community size, and of human loss, written as the possibilities of shifting forms across the island's terrain. The geology of the gneiss is metamorphic.

In the hands of Meades and Boyd this landscape collapses time and space. Not clock-time, biblical time, archaeological phases, or the Mercator projection, but something closer to the vertigo evoked by WG Sebald's commentary on Thomas Browne's *Hydriotaphia* (1658), through which the antiquary's melancholic account of the excavation of particles of cremated human bone in earthenware vessels buried shallow in the Norfolk soil hints that in the practice of archaeology 'the more the distance grows, the clearer the view becomes':

> You glimpse the tiniest details with the utmost clarity. It is as if you were looking through a reversed telescope and through a microscope at the same time.[6]

Towards the close of Meades' text the figure of the future archaeologist appears, discovering modern remains, millennia from now. But the words and images of this book are not about a landscape of modern ruin and fragments of time: they trace the scattered re-wilding of human memory across the topography of Scotland's largest island. Meades' text is stripped away here from the moving image of film; Boyd's photographs are the very opposite of stills. The Isle of Rust, like any relatively remote location, and like the iron in the yellow sand bank at Camas Uig (where 93 12th-century Norse chess pieces carved from walrus ivory and whale teeth were found in 1831) is an ongoing transformation. Against any liquidation of the false consciousness of invented tradition, this double consciousness breathes humanity into the landscape, present into past. As if we might envision an Iron Age not as some fixed past reservoir of time but a vast, open, distant, enduring atmosphere. A remote knowledge emerges through this kind of visual archaeology. And the event-density that it reveals is an index not so much of what has been or what is now, but of what appears to have been.

Endnotes

1. Hugh Trevor-Roper, 1983. The Invention of Tradition: the Highland tradition of Scotland. In E Hobsbawm and T Ranger (eds) *The Invention of Tradition*. Cambridge: CUP, p. 15.
2. Neal Ascherton, 2010. Liquidator. *London Review of Books* 32(16): 10–12.
3. Hugh Trevor-Roper, 1980. History and Imagination. *Times Literary Supplement* 4035 (25 July), p. 833.
4. Derek Cooper, 1985. *The Road to Mingulay. A View of the Western Isles*. London: Routledge and Kegan Paul, p. 182.
5. Robert Smithson, 1995 [1972]. Hotel Palenque. Reproduced in *Parkett* 43: insert (unpaginated).
6. See discussion in Dan Hicks 2019. The Transformation of Visual Archaeology (Part One). In Lesley McFadyen and Dan Hicks (eds) *Archaeology and Photography*. London: Bloomsbury, pp. 21–54.

East German Trabant, Flesherin, Lewis

Luath Press Limited

committed to publishing well written books worth reading

LUATH PRESS takes its name from Robert Burns, whose little collie Luath (*Gael.*, swift or nimble) tripped up Jean Armour at a wedding and gave him the chance to speak to the woman who was to be his wife and the abiding love of his life. Burns called one of the 'Twa Dogs' Luath after Cuchullin's hunting dog in Ossian's *Fingal*. Luath Press was established in 1981 in the heart of Burns country, and is now based a few steps up the road from Burns' first lodgings on Edinburgh's Royal Mile. Luath offers you distinctive writing with a hint of unexpected pleasures.

Most bookshops in the UK, the US, Canada, Australia, New Zealand and parts of Europe, either carry our books in stock or can order them for you. To order direct from us, please send a £sterling cheque, postal order, international money order or your credit card details (number, address of cardholder and expiry date) to us at the address below. Please add post and packing as follows: UK – £1.00 per delivery address; overseas surface mail – £2.50 per delivery address; overseas airmail – £3.50 for the first book to each delivery address, plus £1.00 for each additional book by airmail to the same address. If your order is a gift, we will happily enclose your card or message at no extra charge.

Luath Press Limited
543/2 Castlehill
The Royal Mile
Edinburgh EH1 2ND
Scotland
Telephone: +44 (0)131 225 4326 (24 hours)
Email: sales@luath.co.uk
Website: www.luath.co.uk